LSR Adventure
Stage 3

SURVI̶
SAVAGE SEA

Dougal Robertson/Roy Kingsbury

'Water, water, everywhere,
And all the boards did shrink;
Water, water, everywhere,
Nor any drop to drink.'

(from *The Ancient Mariner*
        Samuel Taylor Coleridge, 1798)

Longman

Longman Group Limited
Longman House, Burnt Mill, Harlow,
Essex CM20 2JE, England
Associated Companies throughout the world

This edition © Longman Group Ltd. 1978

First published 1978
This impression 1984

ISBN 0 582 53691 X

Acknowledgements

We would like to thank Mr Dougal Robertson and his publishers, Elek Books Ltd,
for allowing us to draw heavily on Mr Robertson's own account of the family's ordeal
in his book *Survive The Savage Sea* (first published by Elek Books Ltd, 1973,
subsequently published by Penguin Books Ltd, 1974/1975).

We are grateful to Elek Books for supplying material, and for granting us permission
to reproduce copyright photographs on the cover, and pages 1, 8/9, 46, and 47.

We are grateful to Wayne Reid, of Windsor Safari Park for the photograph of the
killer whale on page 7.

We are also grateful to the following for permission to reproduce copyright material:
Seaphot Pictures for pages 14, 22 (bottom), and 26/27; Nigel Merret at the Institute
of Oceanographic Sciences for page 18; John Norris-Wood for page 22 (top); Heather
Angel (Biofotos) for pages 24, 32 and 33; Ardea for pages 28 and 29; and Mr J.C.
Gibson for pages 40/41. Our thanks also to the National Meteorological Office
Library for supplying the photograph on pages 40/41, and to the Sunday Telegraph
for supplying the newspaper cutting on page 47.

Illustrated by Trevor Parkin (artist's impressions), David Lightfoot (diagrams) and
Pamela Littlewood.

Printed in Hong Kong by
Yu Luen Offset Printing Factory Ltd

SURVIVE THE SAVAGE SEA

'Abandon ship!'

It all happened very quickly. Dougal
Robertson was studying a sea chart. His
wife, Lyn, was cleaning up the schooner.
On deck, Sandy, one of the twin boys,
was fishing. Douglas, Dougal's 17-year-
old son, was steering. Neil, Sandy's twin
brother, was resting in the cabin. Robin,
the 22-year-old student, was resting there,
too.

The 13-metre
schooner Lucette.

The time: approximately 09hrs 55 mins.
The date: June 15, 1972.
The place: 250 kilometres south-west of the Galapagos Islands in the South Pacific.

Their position on the chart: 1°15′ south of the equator, 94°50′ west.

The ship: the *Lucette*, a 13-metre schooner.

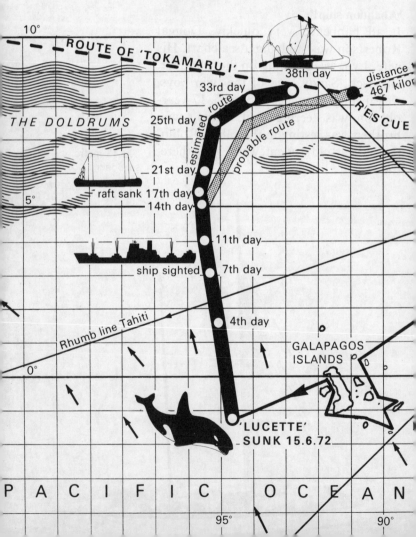

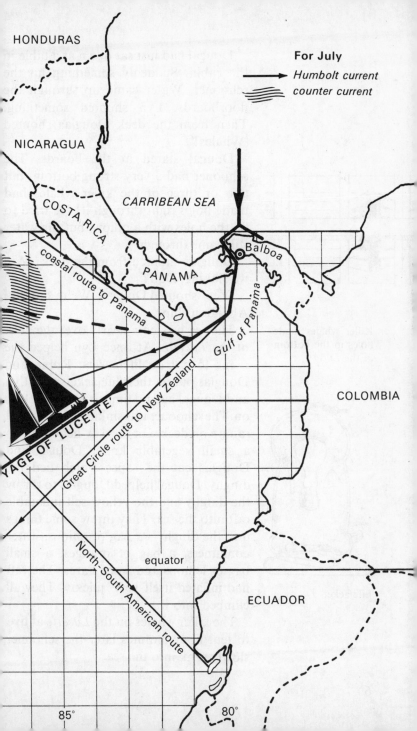

HONDURAS

NICARAGUA

For July
→ Humbolt current
〜 counter current

CARRIBEAN SEA

COSTA RICA

PANAMA

⊙ Balboa

coastal route to Panama

Gulf of Panama

COLOMBIA

Great Circle route to New Zealand

VOYAGE OF 'LUCETTE'

North-South American route

equator

ECUADOR

85°

80°

Dougal had just sat down at a table in the cabin. Suddenly something hit the schooner. Water came up through the floorboards. Lyn shouted something. Then from the deck Douglas shouted 'Whales!'

Dougal stared at the boards. The schooner had a very strong bottom, but two or three of the killer whales had made holes right through it! He tried to fill the holes with a pillow, but the water still came through.

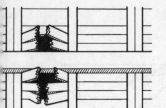

Killer whales made holes in the bottom of the *Lucette*.

Douglas shouted from the deck: 'Are we sinking, Dad?'

'Yes,' shouted Dougal. 'We're sinking! Abandon ship!'

The sea was now nearly over the deck of the *Lucette*. At once Lyn helped the twins to put on lifejackets. Robin and Douglas put on their lifejackets too. Lyn and Dougal had no time to put lifejackets on. The schooner was sinking fast. Dougal ran up on deck. On the way he picked up a small vegetable knife. Dougal and Douglas cut the ropes which tied the dinghy. Dougal helped Douglas to throw the dinghy and the yellow self-inflatable raft into the sea. They threw some things into the dinghy—a bag of onions, water containers, a bag of oranges, a small bag of lemons and some flares. The raft had inflated itself very quickly. They all climbed into it.

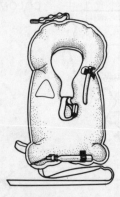

Lifejacket.

The killer whales hit the *Lucette* at five to ten. Four minutes later the schooner slowly sank into the sea.

Killer whales

They all just sat in the raft. It had all happened too quickly. They were alive. But this was just the beginning...

'Let's buy a boat and go round the world'
But what were they doing in the South Pacific—the family with 11-year-old twins, and a student?

Four years before, the family had lived on a farm near Leek in North Staffordshire, England. Dougal Robertson had once been a sea captain. But for the past 15 years he had been a farmer. In 1968, the trouble for many farmers was money. It was for the Robertsons, too.

The Robertson family before leaving England.

One Sunday morning the family was listening to the news. There was a report about the Round-the-World yacht race. Dougal talked about the sea, and he and Lyn described their sailing adventures in Hong Kong.

Suddenly Neil said 'Daddy's a sailor. Why can't we go round the world?'

Lyn laughed. 'What a lovely idea!' she said. 'Let's buy a boat and go round the world.'

It was just a game that Sunday morning. 'But why not?' thought Dougal. 'Why not sail round the world?'

The game became reality. Two years later, they bought the 50-year-old schooner *Lucette* in Malta and sailed her back to Falmouth.

The family left Falmouth in January 1971. Lyn and Dougal had an 18-year-old daughter, Anne. She was with them, too.

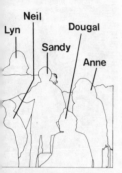

Neil
Lyn
Dougal
Sandy
Anne

Their round-the-world voyage had begun.

They sailed first to Lisbon, then to the Canary Islands. Lyn's sisters, Edna and Mary, flew out from Britain to Las Palmas to say goodbye.

They crossed the Atlantic to the West Indies, then sailed up through the Bahamas to Miami. There they bought a fibreglass dinghy. Lyn's sisters' names were Edna and Mary, so they named the dinghy *Ednamair*. They did not know it, but the dinghy was going to save their lives.

February 1972: Anne fell in love and stayed in Nassau. The others sailed to Jamaica, then to the San Blas Islands and Colon in Panama. There they met Robin Williams, a Welsh student. He asked them to take him with them on the voyage to New Zealand. They said yes.

They sailed through the Panama Canal in May and out into the Bay of Panama. They reached the Galapagos Islands two weeks later. There they visited the islands of Marchena, Chatham, Hood, Isabela and Fernandina. They saw all the strange animals and birds that Darwin had seen and described.

The food rescued from the Lucette.

On June 13 they were ready to leave. When they sailed away from Cape Espinosa, they thought that they had a 4,500-kilometre voyage to the Marquesas Islands in the west.

Instead . . .

Day 1 (June 15) *estimated position 1°15′ south of the equator, 320 kilometres west of Longitude of Espinosa*

It had all happened too quickly. They sat in the raft under the yellow canopy. Neil and Sandy cried quietly. Lyn prayed and sang a hymn. Douglas and Robin watched the sea for things from the *Lucette*. The dinghy *Ednamair* floated a few metres away. Dougal had already fixed it to the raft with a line. The killer whales had gone. But they could not see a ship.

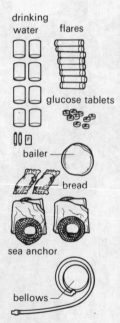

drinking water   flares

glucose tablets

bailer

bread

sea anchor

bellows

Something floated near: it was Lyn's sewing basket. They picked it out of the water, and also some other things—some empty boxes, the canvas raft cover and a plastic cup. All these things were important now.

Dougal put his arm round Neil. 'It's all right now, son,' he said. 'We're safe, and the whales have gone.' Perhaps the whales had gone, but the boys cried. They were crying because the *Lucette* had gone too.

They opened the raft's survival kit and found:

- Bread and glucose for ten men for two days.
- Eight litres of water and eight flares.
- One bailer, four fish-hooks and a fishing line.
- A knife, a mirror, a torch and a first-aid box.
- Two sea anchors, an instruction book, bellows and three paddles.

They also had 12 onions, 10 oranges, 6 lemons, half a kilo of biscuits and a quarter kilo of glucose sweets. It was not very much.

The raft's survival kit.

hooks

first-aid box

mirror
uction book

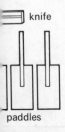
knife

paddles

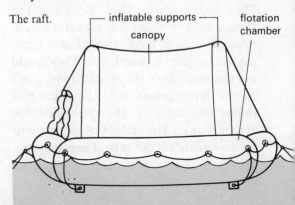
The raft.
inflatable supports
canopy
flotation chamber

Lyn looked at Dougal. 'We must get these boys to land,' she said. 'If we do nothing else with our lives, we must get them to land!'

'Of course,' Dougal said. 'We'll get them to land.'

But how? What could they do? Dougal had to decide.

- They could not row back 320 kilometres against the Humboldt Current to the Galapagos Islands.
- They could not possibly row across the Pacific, so they could not reach the Marquesas Islands.
- Could they reach Central America, 1,600 kilometres to the north-east across the Doldrums?
- Ought they to stay there and wait for rescue?

First evening's supper.

Dougal thought: 'Nobody is looking for us so we can't wait for rescue. Perhaps we'll live for ten days. But after that?' The others waited. Dougal decided. 'We'll stay here for 24 hours,' he said, 'then we must sail north and hope to find rain in the Doldrums.'

Genoa sail.

They knew now that they had a chance. They began work. They looked at the things in Lyn's sewing basket—string, needles, plastic bags, two plastic cups, aspirin, a pen, a pencil, etc. They could use them all. Then they took the wire out of the large genoa sail. (Douglas had pulled the sail into the raft when the *Lucette* sank.) They could use the wire to fix *Ednamair* to the raft. Then they cut up the large sail for a sail for the dinghy, and for bed sheets. They needed bed sheets to keep warm at night. When the *Lucette* sank, they were only wearing swimming shorts and shirts. They had no other clothes.

The raft rose and fell in waves five metres high. Neil and Robin were both already seasick, and Lyn gave them some pills from the first-aid box. Lyn was a nurse. She knew what pills to give them. For the others, supper that first evening was one biscuit, one mouthful of water and one sweet each, and an orange between them. The sun set and it got colder. Lyn prayed again. There was very little room, but they all lay down and tried to rest.

While the others tried to sleep, Dougal estimated their position. He had no compass or chart but he knew that their latitude was 1°15′ south of the equator. He did *not* know their longitude, but after some thought he estimated that the longitude of Espinosa was about 91°20′ west. They were about 320 kilometres west of that.

position of sail
on schooner

12-metre wire

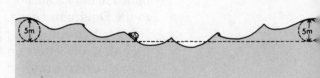

'The raft rose and fell in the waves.'

13

Dorados.

Letter written by Douglas on a piece of genoa sail.

Day 2 (June 16) *1° south, 320 kilometres west of Espinosa*

They did not sleep well that first night. Large fish hit the bottom of the raft all night. (Douglas thought they were dorados.) And no one had enough room to move.

In the night the flotation chamber lost a lot of air, so they tried to pump it up with the bellows. This did not work, so they cut off the bellows tube and blew it up by mouth. Soon the raft was all right again.

Breakfast was a biscuit, a piece of onion and a mouthful of water each. Robin and Neil were still seasick and only had water with their pills from the first-aid box.

That day Lyn, Robin and Sandy cleaned up the raft. Douglas and Dougal bailed water out of the *Ednamair* and put up a sail. The dinghy was going to pull the raft. (While they were bailing, Douglas found his Timex watch in the bottom of the dinghy. It still worked! The vegetable knife was there too. Dougal had thrown it in when the *Lucette* sank.)

Dougal estimated their position. Then at two o'clock in the afternoon Douglas pulled in the sea anchor, and their voyage to the Doldrums began.

Later Lyn cut small pieces of sail and they all wrote letters on them. The twins and Douglas wrote to friends; Robin wrote to his mother; and Lyn and Dougal wrote to Anne. Then they put the letters

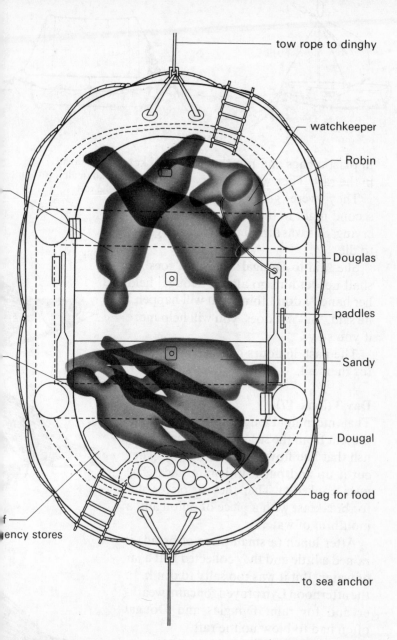

tow rope to dinghy

watchkeeper

Robin

Douglas

paddles

Sandy

Dougal

bag for food

f

ency stores

to sea anchor

The six people asleep in the raft.

15

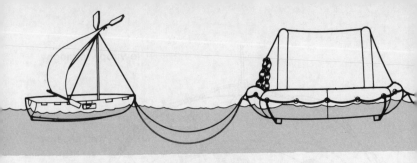

in plastic bags and put them in a pocket in the raft. They were all very sad.

They were getting ready for their second night in the raft. Lyn was almost crying. She was afraid that Neil was going to die.

She said to Dougal: 'If Neil "goes", I shall not let him go alone.' Dougal held her hand. 'I don't think that will happen,' he said, 'but if it does, you will help more if you stay.'

The past 36 hours had been very hard for them all.

Day 3 (June 17)

That morning Dougal found their first present from the sea. It was a small flying fish that had flown into the dinghy. They cut it up and put it in lemon juice. The juice 'cooked' it. Then they ate pieces of it for breakfast with a piece of onion and a mouthful of water.

After lunch (a small piece of bread) it rained a little and they collected half a jar of water. But it was too salty to drink. In the afternoon Lyn prayed for calm weather and for rain. Douglas and Dougal often had to blow up the raft.

At supper time Dougal said: 'We must

The dinghy Ednamair—towing the raft.

Flying fish.

16

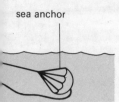
sea anchor

drink only a litre a day between us. We have only twelve tins left and it is 500 kilometres to the Doldrums.'

He looked at the twins sadly. Often that night he heard Lyn's voice in his head: 'We must get these boys to land.'

Day 4 (June 18) *1°18' north, 350 kilometres west of Espinosa*

In the morning there was a clear sky and the promise of a hot day. When Dougal climbed into *Ednamair*, he found two flying fish. There was not enough lemon juice to 'cook' the fish. So they ate it raw with a piece of onion and a piece of orange. They ate each piece very slowly.

Dougal wanted to catch a dorado, so he went back into *Ednamair* and tried the fishing line. But he lost the line and did not catch anything later with another line.

In the afternoon they all rested. It was very, very hot. The twins drew pictures of the *Lucette* and the whales. Lyn wrote a note in cotton on a piece of sail. Dougal drew a sea chart and showed it to the others. 'About 400 kilometres, and then rain,' he said. '400 kilometres at 80 kilometres a day. Five days, and we have ten tins of water left. We'll just be all right.'

The raft was now losing a lot of air. They had to blow up the flotation chambers every 15 minutes in the night. They were still quite fit, but they were already getting thin.

Day 5 (June 19) *2°06′ north, 370 kilometres west of Epinosa*

The morning was beautiful—the sky and sea full of beautiful colours. They were still alive and fit, and two more flying fish came from the sea.

That morning they had a small piece of raw fish for breakfast.

They looked for holes in the flotation chambers. There were some small ones. But Dougal found the real trouble—a small hole in the side. He filled it with a piece of rubber.

In the afternoon they played a game of Twenty Questions. One person thinks of something: the others ask questions to find out the name of the thing. They can only ask 20 questions. The twins liked this game and were very good at it.

It rained in the evening, but they only collected a cup of water. In their wet clothes and bed sheets they got ready for their fifth night in the raft.

Dougal hardly slept at all. His head was full of questions. 'How can we catch

'A large dorado jumped into the dinghy.'

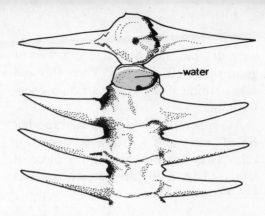

water

Getting water from the vertebrae of a dorado.

fish? How can we get more water? What will happen to us when . . . ?'

Day 6 (June 20) *2°40′ north, 385 kilo-metres west of Espinosa*
At two in the morning a large dorado jumped into the dinghy. Dougal climbed in and killed it with a knife. Then at four o'clock a flying fish came into the raft and hit Lyn's face. They had a good breakfast that day.

In daylight Dougal cut up the dorado and hung pieces up to dry on lines. Then they broke the vertebrae and drank the water from them.

Dougal tried to catch fish again. This time a shark took his line. It was not the first shark they had seen.

After five days, their clothes began to come to pieces. And their bodies began to suffer, too. Neil and Douglas suffered with raw sores on their legs and bottoms. Their faces were thinner too and Douglas had black circles round his eyes.

It was a very hot day. Their mouths

19

were dry but they only had four tins of good water left. The boys knew this and said nothing. They were glad when evening came.

At supper time Dougal opened another tin of water and Lyn prayed again for rain. They ate raw fish and a piece of lemon. That night they dreamed about ice cream and fruit ...

Day 7 (June 21) *3° north, 385 kilometres west of Espinosa*

This was a big day for the Robertsons. It was a day they will not forget.

It began well. It rained heavily. They opened their dry mouths to catch the rain. They filled their tins and plastic bags. They drank, and they washed the salt from their bodies.

Suddenly Douglas pointed and shouted: 'A ship! A ship!'

They all looked.

'Get me the flares,' Dougal said. One flare went up. The ship did not turn. Dougal lit a red hand flare—then another.

'Look! Look!' the boys shouted. The ship sailed on. Nobody was looking.

'They won't see us now,' Dougal said. 'I'm sorry, boys.'

After lunch Dougal said : 'From now on we have a new password. We forget words like rescue. We just think of survival. Remember. Not rescue—survival!'

Lyn asked the twins: 'What's the password for today?'

'Survival!' they both shouted.

'A ship! A ship!'

21

A green turtle.

broken kitchen knife

handle

Turtle knife

Never far away—
the hammerheaded,
man-eating shark.

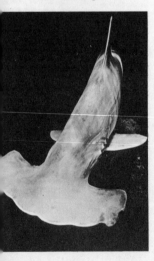

Dougal decided to stay in the Panama-Marquesas shipping route for 48 hours. There was the chance of another ship.

Late in the afternoon a large turtle hit the raft. 'We'll have this one,' Dougal said. 'Let's pull it into the dinghy.' And soon the 40-kilo turtle was lying on its back in the bottom of the dinghy.

Now Dougal had to kill it. He put one foot on one front flipper, and his other foot on the other flipper. He held the turtle's beak in his left hand and cut through its neck with the sharp knife. Blood filled the bottom of the dinghy and the turtle died. There was red blood on Dougal's clothes. It did not matter. The password now was Survival! 'The strongest live; the weakest die.' The Robertsons had become savages in a savage sea.

Day 8 (June 22) *3° north, 385 kilometres west of Espinosa*

In the morning Dougal went over to the dinghy to cut up the turtle. It was a hard job. It took him an hour and a half. The turtle was a female and there were a lot of eggs inside her. Breakfast that morning was different—and very good: raw turtle meat and eggs!

Several times in the day Dougal climbed into *Ednamair* to turn the pieces of turtle meat. The ten kilos of meat quickly dried in the sun.

Lyn had a lot to do as well. She had to look after their health. They lay and sat in salt water a lot of the time, and their

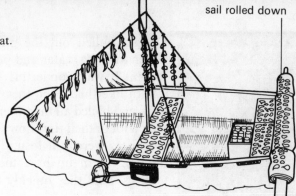

sail rolled down

Drying the meat.

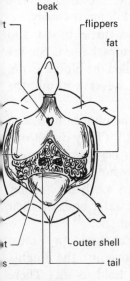

beak

flippers

fat

outer shell

tail

Underside of a female turtle.

bodies often touched the canvas of the raft—so their sores and boils got worse. The sores and boils hurt a lot and their health was getting worse.

That night Dougal's head was full of questions again:

'We have food and water, but will the raft last a long time? How often will we catch a turtle? The oranges and lemons are nearly finished. How long can we live without vitamin C?'

He had no books to tell him the answers.

Day 9 (June 23) *3°10′ north, 387 kilometres west of Espinosa*

The day was *very* hot. They were under the canopy, but they could feel the midday sun. They were resting in the afternoon when Dougal's hand touched the plug in the bottom of the raft. They could not swim in the sea: there were always sharks. But he suddenly had an idea. 'Come on,' he said. 'We're going to have a bath.' And to Robin: 'You first!'

23

White-tipped shark —'they were never without the sharks'

Dougal pulled out the plug, filled the bailer with sea water and poured it over Robin. It was wonderful! They all had a bath like this. Then they put the plug back and bailed all the water out. Bailing took a lot of their time now. The flotation chambers were still losing a lot of air. Blowing them up hurt their dry, sore mouths. And they quickly became tired as well.

Day 10 (June 24) *3°30′ north, 400 kilometres west of Espinosa*
They had stayed two days in the shipping route, but had not seen another ship. Douglas pulled in the sea anchor, Dougal opened *Ednamair's* sail, and they began to sail towards the Doldrums. The Doldrums were 150 kilometres away.

Dougal threw the turtle blood and other turtle pieces into the sea. Sharks came. They had smelled the blood. From then on they were never without the sharks.

In the afternoon the plug came out of the bottom of the raft. (They didn't pull it out. The raft was beginning to wear badly.) They filled the hole with a dinghy instruction book. This was bad. *And* they all suffered with salt water boils on their arms, legs and bottoms.

'Soon,' thought Dougal, 'we must leave the raft and move into the dinghy. But will the dinghy hold us all? There are six of us and the dinghy is less than three metres long!'

Day 11 (June 25) *4° north, 400 kilometres west of Espinosa*

They ate the last pieces of lemon and onion. 'When will it rain again?' they asked. 'In two days? In a week? Who knows?'

Douglas cleaned the turtle shell. He and Dougal put their fish meat in a box. They used the turtle shell for a cover.

In the afternoon Dougal began to make a fish spear from a piece of wood from a box. He was still making it when night came.

That night he and Sandy slept in the dinghy, but they had little sleep. The dinghy was very hard. The raft was beginning to wear badly, but it was still better and softer than the dinghy.

Day 12 (June 26) was like many days before. They bailed almost all the time. But they did things more slowly now, and Lyn shouted at them. She prayed again for rain, and when Robin said something funny about prayers, Dougal nearly hit him. Robin said he was sorry and Dougal went into *Ednamair* again to try and catch fish with his spear. But he hit it against the mast and broke it, so he could not use it. Dougal was very angry with himself.

Late that night a large fish jumped against the side of the raft. When it jumped again, Dougal put his arm round it and began to pull it out of the water. He looked down. He was holding a one-

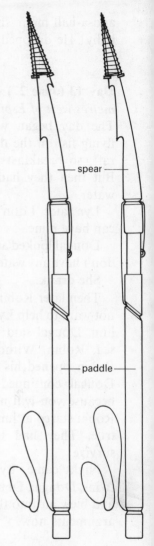

spear

paddle

Dougal made fish spears.

VISTA

and-a-half metre shark in his arms like a baby! He dropped it like a hot potato!

Day 13 (June 27) *4°45′ north, 400 kilometres west of Espinosa*
The day began well. There were two flying fish in the dinghy and one in the raft, so breakfast was half a fish each. But then they had an argument about water.

Lyn said: 'I don't want any. The twins can have mine.'

Dougal looked at her and said: 'If you don't have any water, we won't have any.'

She drank.

Then later Robin became lazy. He did not want to help Lyn. She was angry with him. Dougal said: 'You are new to the sea, Robin. Without us, you will die.' Robin opened his mouth to speak. But Dougal continued: 'If one of us dies because you will not help, *I'll kill you!*' Robin stared at him. He could see it was true. They had to work together to survive!

Night came. Lyn told stories to the twins. Dougal, Douglas and Robin bailed and blew air into the raft. There were no arguments now.

Day 14 (June 28) *5° north, 400 kilometres west of Espinosa*
The raft was in a poor condition now. There were a lot of holes. Sandy found a big one and Dougal tried to fill it, but he

26

Mako shark.

could not. 'We'll have to bail all the time now,' he thought. 'And the raft can't last. We *must* move into the dinghy soon.'

Suddenly Sandy shouted 'Turtle!' They caught it and pulled it into the dinghy. Dougal cut through its neck.

'Catch the blood!' Lyn called. 'It ought to be all right to drink a little.' And it was. They all drank some.

They had now reached the Doldrums. The sun was very hot. There were no clouds or wind and they had only four tins of water left. Their boils and sores were worse now. They had all got very thin too and they were in poor health.

That evening they drank no water. But they still had to bail out the sea water and blow air into the raft. They could not sleep in the sea water.

'We must abandon the raft soon,' Dougal thought. 'It's slowly killing us.'

They had been in the raft for two weeks.

Day 15 (June 29) *5°15′ north, 400 kilometres west of Espinosa*

It rained at dawn. They collected nearly 15 litres, and drank and drank. It was wonderful.

The twins were talking when they heard Douglas: 'Dad, the dinghy's gone!' The line had broken. The dinghy was 60 metres away. Dougal moved fast. The dinghy was their only hope—it was their lives. He dived into the sea and swam hard. Douglas shouted 'Shark!' but Dougal swam harder. The shark followed him. The others could only watch and hope. 'He's done it!' Douglas shouted. Dougal had reached the dinghy. 'Good old Dad,' shouted Sandy.

Dougal paddled back to the raft and fixed the dinghy to it again. He was very, very tired. Lyn gave him some water and a piece of glucose, and held him in her arms.

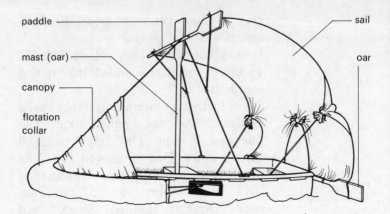

paddle

mast (oar)

canopy

flotation
collar

sail

oar

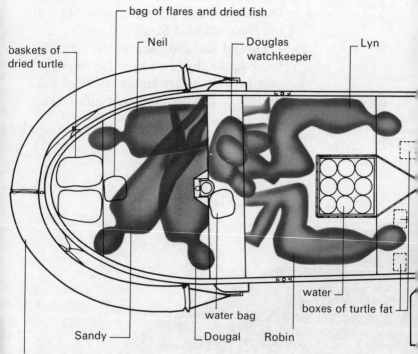

bag of flares and dried fish

baskets of
dried turtle

Neil

Douglas
watchkeeper

Lyn

Sandy

water bag

Dougal

Robin

water

boxes of turtle fat

flotation collar

Day 16 (June 30) *5°15′ north. 400 kilo-metres west of Epinosa*

It rained, cold rain, all night. They bailed the warm sea water out of the raft. They did not sleep much; they lay in water nearly all the time and their sores and boils hurt.

It rained all day, too. They ate dried turtle and fish and drank plenty of water.

It was early evening. Douglas suddenly said 'Quiet! Engines.' They all listened. There was a sound. It got louder. Then nothing. Was it a ship?—or a submarine? They never knew.

That night was very bad. 'We're sinking,' said Lyn. 'The twins will drown in the raft if we fall asleep.' But at last the rain began to stop.

Day 17 (July 1) *5°20′ north, 400 kilo-metres west of Espinosa*

The last night of June was also their last in the raft. The rain had stopped and the sea was calm. In the day they moved things from the raft to the dinghy. The twins, Lyn and Robin climbed carefully into the dinghy first. Then Dougal and Douglas took necessary things from the raft—the canopy and lines and other things. They untied the raft. It floated away and sank. They were sad. It had carried them 650 kilometres but they still had 1,100 kilometres to go. And now they only had *Ednamair* to carry them.

They cleaned up the dinghy, put up a sun canopy, and fixed the flotation collar and a steering oar.

The dinghy was small and it was not easy to move around. It was uncomfortable, but they did not have to blow it up all the time—or bail out water. And the dorados could not hit their bottoms!

Day 18 (July 2) *5°30' north, 393 kilometres west of Espinosa*

The morning was clear and one flying fish had landed in the dinghy in the night. Breakfast again was raw flying fish and turtle. But some meat had gone bad in the rain, so they had to throw it away.

They pulled in the sea anchor and put up the sail. They still had a long way to go. But they felt that they could live in the dinghy. And they felt that they were now going home.

Blue-footed booby.

They had dreamed about food and often talked about it. That day they talked about a restaurant that they wanted to open in Leek. They named it Dougal's Kitchen.

They themselves were now in better condition. Their sores and boils had begun to dry. But their clothes ...

In the evening the wind got stronger and the waves got bigger. They got ready to sleep.

Day 19 (July 3)

It rained in the night and again in the morning. The weather was cold. They took down the sail and began to collect rainwater. They caught it in the canopy

Frigate bird.

and filled the empty water tins.

They did not want all the turtle to go bad, so they ate plenty.

The rain stopped in the afternoon, and they had a visitor. A large sea bird flew down and landed on Douglas's shoulder. They all liked it but Neil said 'Kill it. I'll eat it!' He had become a savage too. They laughed at Neil and let the bird fly away.

Day 20 (July 4) *5°55′ north, 392 kilometres west of Espinosa*
This was Lyn's birthday. They caught another turtle and had a birthday dinner: turtle meat, dry pieces of dorado and plenty of water.

They rested in the afternoon and talked about past birthdays. Then, after a long birthday tea, they sang 'Happy Birthday' and a lot of other songs.

That evening Dougal talked to the twins. He thought it was necessary. He had made a sea chart. 'We're here now,' he explained, 'and we're sailing towards Central America—here. We shall begin to row in a few days. We'll get there in about 35 days.'

Day 21 (July 5) *6° north, 385 kilometres west of Espinosa*
After breakfast the line of the sea anchor broke. They needed the sea anchor. They quickly pulled down the sail and Douglas rowed to fetch it. It took him 35 minutes. It was very hard work. While Dougal

33

fixed the sea anchor again, Lyn gave Douglas some water and glucose.

That evening they thought they saw a green flare. There was no sign of a ship, but they were not sad. Their password now was 'Survival', not 'Rescue'.

Day 22 (July 6) *6°20' north, 385 kilometres west of Espinosa*

That night was better. Dougal slept for three hours—a long time for him. In the morning they caught and killed another big turtle. They drank the blood and had a good lunch. In the afternoon they talked again about Dougal's Kitchen and food.

Dougal watched the sky. Bad weather was coming. They got ready for a storm. In the evening the wind was very strong. Big waves came into the dinghy. They bailed and bailed. And what a storm it was!

Day 23 (July 7) *6°50' north 385, kilometres west of Espinosa*

All night the rain got harder and harder. Suddenly there was no wind. It rained ten times harder than before. Dougal steered, the others bailed. Dougal began to die from cold. Robin stopped bailing and rubbed Dougal's arms and back. Then Douglas shouted! 'Sing! Sing to keep warm!' They sang. And bailed and bailed. Suddenly the wind came back. The dinghy was now half full of water. It nearly sank. But they bailed the water out and they survived the terrible storm.

The storm.

35

When daylight came, they were still bailing—but very slowly. They were all very, very tired. They were still alive, but only just alive. For breakfast they had pieces of turtle meat and a piece of biscuit each. They had prayed for water— but that had been too much. They had nearly died that night.

Day 24 (July 8) *7°40′ north, 370 kilometres west of Espinosa*
It rained all the next night too. Robin and Dougal bailed all night. They became very very tired: they couldn't feel their bodies or any pain. Lyn was very tired too, but she rubbed their arms and legs to bring life back to them. At dawn the rain stopped. The sea was calm. They slept. Douglas kept watch.

In the afternoon the sun came out and they hung up all their clothes to dry. They rested and talked.

Day 25 (July 9) *7°23′ north, 360 kilometres west of Espinosa*
They caught and killed another female turtle that day, then rested. The weather was good now, but very hot.

There were other signs of life, too. Three large sea birds visited them and landed on the dinghy's mast.

The family were happier now. They were alone in the Pacific. But they had found out that they could survive a storm.

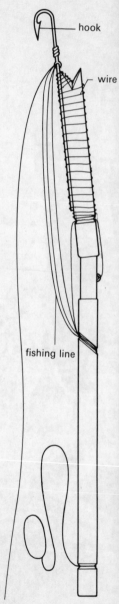

hook

wire

fishing line

Dougal made gaffs.

fishing line

Day 26 (July 10) *7°30′ north, 336 kilometres west of Espinosa*

That day they lost the sea anchor. Perhaps a shark took it. They didn't know. They had another one and Dougal fixed it. The weather was bad and the sea was rough. While the twins were eating their 'little supper' (15 grams of biscuit and a little glucose), the others talked about Dougal's Kitchen. They only had raw fish to eat.

Day 27 (July 11) *7°33′ north, 305 kilometres west of Espinosa*

That afternoon Dougal again tried to catch fish with his spear. He waited and waited, the spear in his hand. When a dorado swam near, Dougal hit it with the spear. The tip broke! The wood was too soft. 'I'll have to make a gaff,' he thought. 'I'll tie a fish hook on the end of the spear, then I can pull the fish in.' He was still working on it when evening came.

Day 28 (July 12) *7°40′ north, 280 kilometres west of Espinosa*

The weather got worse and the sea was very rough. *Ednamair* was heavy in the water and waves came in. Dougal could not understand it. Then he looked at the flotation collar. That was the trouble! It was full of water! He cut off the collar, emptied it, pumped it up and fixed it on again. It had nearly sunk them.

That day Dougal thought. Soon they ought to begin to row. But they needed a calm sea. And they could not row without enough water to drink. They needed a large container, but they did not have one. 'Of course we have!' Dougal thought. 'The flotation collar! If the sea is calm enough to row, we won't need the collar.'

Day 29 (July 13) *7°50′ north, 256 kilometres west of Espinosa*

They had now accepted one thing: they had to kill to eat. Early that morning Dougal was working on his gaff. The sea was quite calm. He looked down and saw a one-and-a-half metre Mako shark under the dinghy. 'Why not try to catch it?' he thought. He put a small flying fish on the large fish hook, held the line and threw it out.

'What are you doing, Dad?' said Douglas.

'Catching a shark,' Dougal said calmly.

'You're mad!' said Lyn and Douglas.

'Good old Dad,' said the twins. But the others thought he was mad.

Dougal felt a pull on the line. The shark bit and Dougal pulled it in. The shark fought hard, but in the end he pulled it to the dinghy. Lyn put the paddle into the shark's jaws. Dougal caught its tail and pulled it into the dinghy. After that he killed it with the knife and cut off its head. Then he cut it up. They had a good meal that day: raw shark meat!

Dougal catches
a shark.

Dougal was not mad. In savage life, shark eats man, or man eats shark! Now, with the shark and the turtle meat, they had enough food to last a week.

Days 30 and 31 (July 14 and 15)

They had food now but very little water. They caught two turtles, but they could only get blood from turtles. And it was hot—very, very hot. The sun shone all day. A person needs a litre of water every day to survive in the hot sun. They only had a litre for six people. They were thirsty, their mouths were always dry, and they only had four litres of water left.

They began to quarrel too. They thought that they had a plastic bag of water. They found it in the bottom of the dinghy—empty. Robin had not tied it properly. They shouted at Robin and they quarrelled. Then, when Dougal used his gaff to try to catch a fish, he lost the hook and broke the line. He was angry. Lyn was, too, and they quarrelled again.

Day 32 (July 16) *8° north, 216 kilometres west of Espinosa*

It was very hot again that day. They only had three litres of water left.

Dougal had finished his second gaff and was ready to try to catch fish with it. Then Lyn began to complain about their life. She complained about their life on the farm, and their condition now. She and Dougal quarrelled. In the end Dougal said: 'Lyn, if you don't be quiet, I'll

'Later they saw rain not far away, but none came.'

40

leave you and go to sea.' A few minutes later he caught a dorado. Now Lyn was happy. 'Thank you, my love,' she said. Dougal was surprised. 'Are you telling me . . . ?' he began. 'Yes,' she replied, and smiled. 'Come on. What are we waiting for? Let's eat!' And they had a good meal of dorado and turtle. They had no water, but drank the water from the vertebrae instead.

Later they saw rain not far away, but none came.

When night came, their mouths were very dry. They were all very thirsty—too thirsty to sleep.

Day 33 (July 17) was another very, very hot day, with no clouds and no sign of rain. They drank a mouthful or two of water each. They got water from the vertebrae and the eyes of three dorados that Dougal caught. Dougal poured salt water on Douglas and Robin. Lyn poured water over the twins. 'Why can't we drink it?' they asked. 'Because it will kill you,' answered Lyn.

That night was bad. They were thirsty. And they thought they saw ships' lights. They were only stars.

Day 34 (July 18) *8°05′ north, 190 kilometres west of Espinosa*
The day began very badly. They had four tins of water left. They had one mouthful each. Dougal caught a fish. It hit Robin's leg and jumped out of the dinghy. Then

Douglas caught a turtle. It was too strong for him. He let it go. Dougal shouted at them.

Late in the afternoon it rained! It was not much, but they collected two cans in the sail. It was better than nothing!

That evening Lyn prayed again for rain. They needed it.

Day 35 (July 19) *8° 10′ north, 185 kilometres west of Espinosa*

Rain came early in the morning. It rained for an hour. It was wonderful! They filled the containers, the tins and the plastic bag. (They let Robin do that.) And they drank and drank. Breakfast was raw turtle and shark meat—and w a t e r!

They saw another turtle. They all said 'Let Dougal catch it.' But Robin tried and let it go. Dougal was very angry. He hit Robin. 'You fool!' he shouted. 'If you do that again, I'll hit you with this paddle!' For Dougal, the head of the family, this was no game. They were fighting the Pacific. They were fighting to live! They needed every turtle and fish they could catch.

Later he took off the flotation collar again. It had holes in it and was half full of water. He cut it in two pieces and held up one half. 'This,' he said, 'is our water tank. It'll hold about 30 litres. When it's half full, we'll begin to row.'

Day 36 (July 20)

Their clothes were now in a very poor

42

condition, so Lyn washed and mended them. They still suffered with salt water boils and sores, and the twins were very thin. But they were all eating and drinking well, and their condition was slowly getting better.

Day 37 (July 21) *8° 15′ north, 150 kilometres west of Espinosa*

The day before had ended cold, wet and windy. In the night Douglas and Dougal had steered, Lyn and Robin had bailed. The rain stopped and they had breakfast.

Suddenly someone shouted 'Turtle!'

Dougal looked at Robin and Douglas. 'This one's mine,' he said. After a long fight they pulled it into the dinghy. It was hard work. Was this turtle stronger than the others?—or were they getting weaker? Perhaps both.

Dougal looked at his chart. He told the others they were now near the Panama-Hawaii shipping route. The others said nothing and this pleased Dougal. Survival was their password now, not Rescue.

They did not have to bail that afternoon. That was good. Fish and turtle pieces were drying on the lines, and they talked again about Dougal's Kitchen.

In the evening Dougal thought land was about 550 kilometres away. That was about 15 days. 'If rain comes and we can fill the collar,' he thought, 'we can begin to row tomorrow.'

Fighting to live!'

Dougal's log.

ELLIOT EQUIPMENT LIMITED
(One of the P. B. Cow Group)
LLWYNYPIA, RHONDDA
SOUTH WALES

ELLIOT EQUIPMENT LIM...

It is most importa...
being dehydrated
first actions there...

These notes a...
to all sizes of...
ance must th...
apparent discr...
to some rafts,...
in them than...
different desig...
IMME...
One of the two lar...
the necessary advic...
to inflate the vario...
adjust the sleeve e...
SE...

Day 38 (July 22)

Day came. It had not rained much in the night. They hung up the pieces of meat to dry. Then Dougal decided to catch some fish. He had decided that they must begin to row the next day, but they had to have enough food.

Dougal caught one dorado. But the next one took the big hook and broke the fishing line. That finished it.

That afternoon Lyn bathed the twins and they went under the canopy.

It was now early evening. Lyn and Dougal were talking about Dougal's Kitchen. Suddenly Dougal stopped and stared. The others looked at him. 'A ship,' he said. 'There's a ship and it's coming towards us!' He stood up in the dinghy. He lit a flare and held it in the air.

'Oh, God,' said Lyn, 'please let them see us.'

Dougal threw the flare into the air. The ship turned towards them. It had seen them.

'Our ordeal is over,' Dougal said quietly. Lyn and the twins cried. They were very happy. Douglas put his arms round his mother. And Robin laughed and cried at the same time. 'Wonderful! We've done it. Wonderful!' he shouted.

Dougal put his arms round Lyn. There were tears in his eyes. They had fought the Pacific and had survived.

'We'll get these boys to land,' he said.

They were safe.

BRITONS SAVED 37 DAYS AFTER WHALE SINKS BOAT

SIX Britons, whose sailing boat collided with a whale and sank 37 days ago, were rescued from a small liferaft yesterday by a Japanese fishing boat in the eastern Pacific, the Maritime Safety Agency said in Tokyo.

The agency said the six Britons were picked up about 660 miles off the coast of Panama by the tuna fishing boat Toka Maru No. 1.

They included the captain, Mr. D. I. Robertson, 48, two children and one woman.

According to a radio message from the 254-ton Japanese vessel, the agency said, the British boat, identified as "Lucette" of London, sank after it collided with a whale about 210 miles off the Galapagos islands on June 15.

In good condition

The rescued Britons were all in good condition, it said. The agency said the Japanese fishing boat was expected to reach Panama on Tuesday. No other details were available.

Whales, the biggest mammals, have been reported several times to have sunk small ocean-going vessels.

A South African sloop sank after being struck by a whale in the Atlantic in January last year.

A 60ft. whale sank a New Zealand ocean-racing yacht in 1968. The crew of seven were saved after spending five days adrift in a dinghy in the Tasman Sea between New Zealand and Australia.—Reuter, A.P.

Neil is carried ashore at Panama.

Rescued by **Japanese seamen** on the Tokamaru 1.

47

Glossary of some technical words used in the story

Abandon ship! = Everybody must leave the ship! A captain shouts this in emergencies, for example when a ship or boat is sinking.

bail (vb) (or **bale**) = to empty water out of a boat with a container of some kind, for example a tin. The thing you use is a **bailer**.

chart (or **sea chart**) = a map of an area of sea.

the Doldrums: An area of sea around the equator. The weather there is usually very sultry. There is often no wind at all. In the past sailors did not want to sail into the area.

flare = a light signal used in emergencies. There are different kinds. You hold some in your hand; you shoot others into the air with a pistol.

flotation chamber/flotation collar: That part of an inflatable raft (see picture, page 11) which keeps a raft or boat afloat.

Humboldt Current: A sea current which flows north along the coast of Chile and Peru. It is a cold current which produces low air temperatures and quite a lot of fog and rain.

line = a rope used at sea, for example to tie one boat to another, in order to pull it.

sea anchor: A kind of floating anchor fixed to a boat to keep it steady. (see picture, page 16)

steering oar: An oar used (instead of a rudder) to steer a boat.